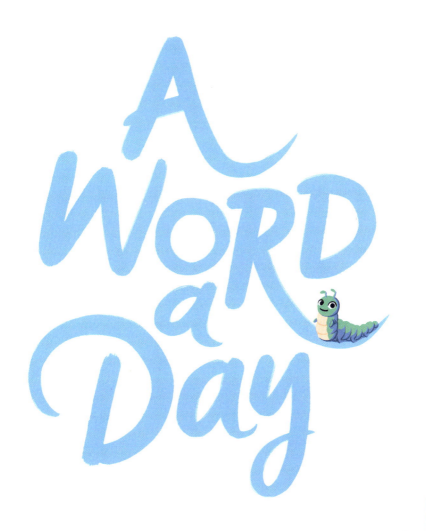

Published by Collins
An imprint of HarperCollins Publishers
Westerhill Road
Bishopbriggs
Glasgow G64 2QT

www.collins.co.uk

HarperCollins Publishers
1st Floor, Watermarque Building, Ringsend Road, Dublin 4, Ireland

First published 2022

A catalogue record for this book is available from the British Library.

ISBN   978-0-00-854584-0

Printed in India

10 9 8 7 6 5 4 3 2 1

Acknowledgements
Publisher: Michelle I'Anson • Editor: Beth Ralston
Designer: Kevin Robbins • Illustrator: Julia Murray
Typesetter: Jouve • Word list curated by Deborah Friedland
With special thanks to Maree Airlie, Mary O'Neill and Gina Macleod

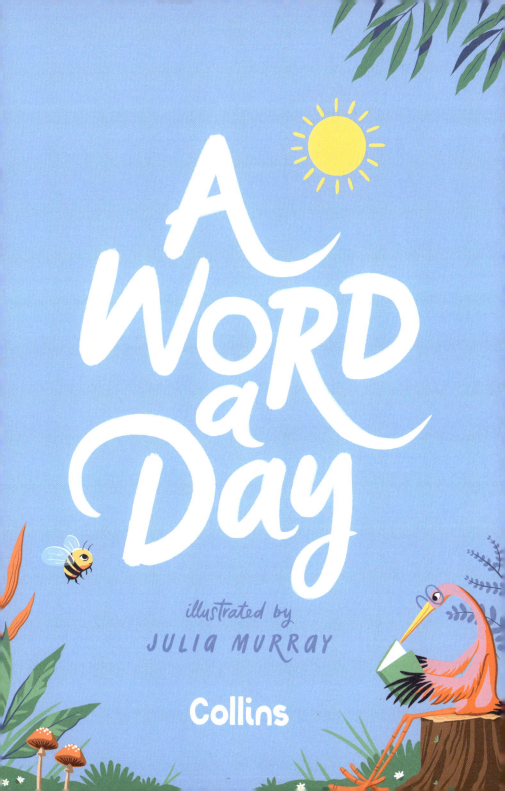

A Word a Day

illustrated by
JULIA MURRAY

Collins

WELCOME LITTLE LOGOPHILES!

A **logophile** (that's you!) is someone who loves words, and your **vocabulary** is all the words you know.

The bigger your vocabulary, the more you will understand about the world. This means that words are valuable and powerful – but they can also be a lot of fun!

In this book you will find all kinds of weird and wonderful words – from the serious to the downright silly and everything in-between – alongside what they mean, hints on how to say them out loud, and lots of colourful pictures.

Do you know what **loquacious** means? What about **anthropomorphise**, **kerfuffle** or **phantasmagorical**? Well, you're about to!

Because your year of discovery is about to begin.

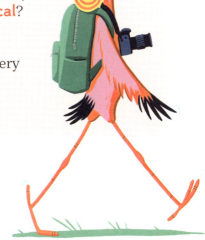

HOW TO READ THIS BOOK

In this book you will find a new and exciting word for every day of the year, which will look like this:

This is the day of the month.

This is the word of the day.

This is how you pronounce the word. Try sounding it out.

This is the type of word, called the 'part of speech'.

1st

demonstration

de-mon-stray-shun

NOUN

A demonstration shows you how something works.

* Demonstration comes from the Latin word 'demonstrare', which means 'point out'.

This is what the word means, called the 'definition'.

This is where the word comes from, called the 'etymology'.

EACH MONTH YOU'LL SPOT BUBBLES LIKE THESE BESIDE SOME OF THE WORDS. THESE ARE **SPECIAL EVENTS AND FESTIVALS!**

A word's part of speech tells you how it is used in a sentence:

1.
noun

A noun is a word used to talk about a person, place, or thing. 'Sister', 'beach' and 'cat' are all nouns.

2.
verb

A verb is a word used to talk about an action. 'Jump', 'whistle' and 'eat' are all verbs.

3.
adjective

An adjective is a word used to describe a noun. 'Clever', 'sunny' and 'orange' are all adjectives.

4.
adverb

An adverb is a word used to describe a verb. 'Quickly', 'happily' and 'greedily' are all adverbs.

ONE OF THE MONTHS HAS AN EXTRA SPECIAL **BONUS WORD!** CAN YOU GUESS WHICH MONTH THAT MIGHT BE?

Also, keep an eye out for the Word Bird who will appear once every month next to their favourite word!

is for

JANUARY

1st
resolution
res-a-loo-shun

NOUN

A resolution is a promise you make to yourself to do something, often at the start of a new year.

2nd
tectonic
tek-ton-ik

ADJECTIVE

Tectonic is a word that you use when you are talking about the structure of the Earth's crust.

3rd
ditto
dit-to

NOUN

You can use the word ditto to agree with something that has just been said, or to avoid repeating it.

* Ditto comes from the Italian word 'detto', which means 'said before'.

4th
emboss
em-boss

VERB

If you emboss a surface such as paper or wood with a design, you make the design stand up slightly from the surface.

TODAY IS WORLD BRAILLE DAY. BRAILLE IS A WRITING SYSTEM FOR BLIND PEOPLE USING RAISED DOTS THAT CAN BE FELT ON THE PAGE.

5th
masquerade
mask-ur-ayd

NOUN

A masquerade is an event, such as a party or dance, where people dress up in disguise and wear masks.

6th
auditorium
awe-di-tor-ee-um

NOUN

The auditorium is the part of a theatre or concert hall where the audience sits.

7th
nostalgia
nost-al-juh

NOUN

Nostalgia is an affectionate feeling you have for the past, especially for a particularly happy time.

8th
octave
oc-tiv

NOUN

An octave is a series of eight notes in music.

* Octave comes from the Latin word 'octo', which means 'eight'.

11

9th
unfathomable
un-fath-um-a-bul

ADJECTIVE

If you say that something is unfathomable, you mean that it cannot be understood or explained, usually because it is very strange or complicated.

10th
aurora
awe-raw-ra

NOUN

An aurora is a dazzling display of coloured light, usually green, red, purple or yellow, that sometimes moves across the sky at night.

11th
prevaricate
pre-var-i-kayt

VERB

If you prevaricate, you avoid giving a direct answer or making a firm decision.

12th
ibis
eye-bis

NOUN

An ibis is a long-legged wading bird with a long, thin bill, typically found in warm parts of the world.

* Ibis comes from a word in the ancient Egyptian language. The Egyptians thought the ibis was a sacred bird.

13th
bashfully
bash-fu-lee

ADVERB

If you say something bashfully, you say it shyly.

14th
kaleidoscopic
kal-eye-di-sko-pik

ADJECTIVE

If you describe something as kaleidoscopic, you mean that it is made up of a lot of different colours, patterns or shapes.

TODAY IS UTTARAYAN KITE DAY, WHEN PEOPLE IN GUJARAT, INDIA, FLY COLOURFUL KITES FROM DAWN UNTIL DUSK.

15th
algorithm
al-gor-ith-um

NOUN

An algorithm is a set of mathematical instructions that help to solve a particular problem, especially on a computer.

16th
dazzling
daz-ling

ADJECTIVE

A dazzling light is so bright that you cannot see for a short time after looking at it.

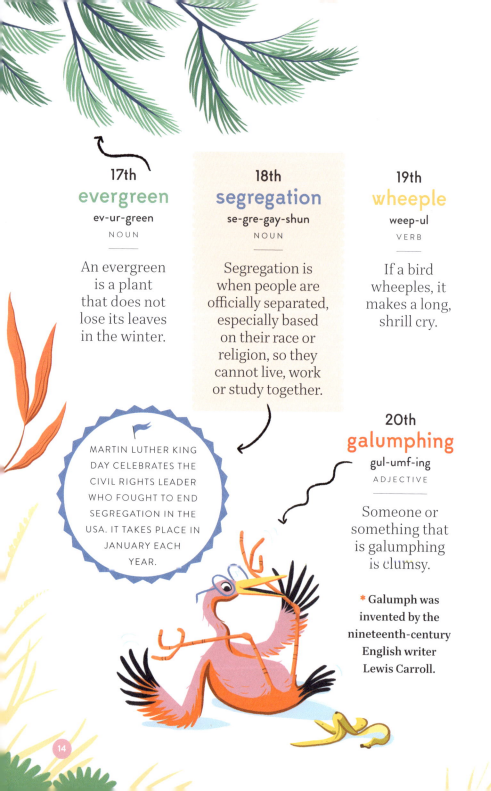

17th
evergreen
ev-ur-green
NOUN

An evergreen is a plant that does not lose its leaves in the winter.

18th
segregation
se-gre-gay-shun
NOUN

Segregation is when people are officially separated, especially based on their race or religion, so they cannot live, work or study together.

19th
wheeple
weep-ul
VERB

If a bird wheeples, it makes a long, shrill cry.

MARTIN LUTHER KING DAY CELEBRATES THE CIVIL RIGHTS LEADER WHO FOUGHT TO END SEGREGATION IN THE USA. IT TAKES PLACE IN JANUARY EACH YEAR.

20th
galumphing
gul-umf-ing
ADJECTIVE

Someone or something that is galumphing is clumsy.

* Galumph was invented by the nineteenth-century English writer Lewis Carroll.

21st
limelight
lime-lite
NOUN

If someone is in the limelight, a lot of attention is being paid to them, because they are famous or because they have done something very unusual or exciting.

22nd
hangry
hang-gree
ADJECTIVE

If someone is hangry, they are grumpy because they are hungry. You use this word in a humorous way.

* **Hangry is a combination of the words 'hungry' and 'angry'.**

23rd
zither
zith-ur
NOUN

A zither is a musical instrument made by stretching strings over a flat box. You pluck the strings with your fingers to make musical notes.

24th
saffron
sa-fron
NOUN

Saffron is a yellowish-orange spice used to colour and flavour food.

* **Saffron comes from a word in the Arabic language.**

JANUARY

25th
sleekit
slee-kit
ADJECTIVE

Sleekit is a Scottish word meaning sly and cunning, just like the crafty field mouse in the Robert Burns poem 'To a Mouse'.

TODAY IS BURNS NIGHT, WHICH CELEBRATES THE BIRTHDAY OF THE FAMOUS SCOTTISH POET, ROBERT BURNS.

27th
dandle
dan-dul
VERB

If you dandle a child, you jiggle them playfully up and down on your knee.

26th
bandicoot
ban-di-koot
NOUN

A bandicoot is a small, furry Australian animal with a long, pointed muzzle and a long tail.

28th
architecture
ar-ki-tek-cher
NOUN

Architecture is the art of designing and constructing buildings, or the style of the building itself.

* Architecture comes from the Greek word 'arkhitekton', which means 'head builder'.

TODAY IS INTERNATIONAL LEGO™ DAY. IT MARKS THE ANNIVERSARY OF THE FIRST LEGO BRICK, WHICH WAS MADE IN 1958.

29th
jabberwock
jab-ber-wok

NOUN

The jabberwock is the fictional monster in Lewis Carroll's poem 'Jabberwocky'.

30th
tapestry
tap-es-tree

NOUN

A tapestry is a large piece of cloth that has a picture woven into it using coloured threads.

31st
perspicacious
per-spik-ay-shus

ADJECTIVE

Someone who is perspicacious is able to notice and understand things quickly.

is for

FEBRUARY

FEBRUARY

1st
blizzard
bliz-urd

NOUN

A blizzard is a very heavy snowstorm with strong winds.

2nd
prototype
pro-to-tipe

NOUN

A prototype is the first example of something, such as a machine or device, which is not yet ready to be sold.

3rd
anthropomorphise
an-thro-pu-morf-ize

VERB

If you anthropomorphise an animal or an object, you treat it as though it has human characteristics or behaviour.

4th
circadian
sur-cayd-ee-un
ADJECTIVE

Circadian is a word used to describe biological events that take place every 24 hours, like going to sleep at night.

*Circadian comes from the Latin words 'circa', which means 'about', and 'dies', which means 'day'.

5th
scintillating
sin-tul-ay-ting
ADJECTIVE

A scintillating conversation is lively and interesting.

*Scintillate comes from the Latin word 'scintilla', which means 'spark'.

6th
abruptly
a-brupt-lee
ADVERB

If you do something abruptly, you do it very suddenly, often in a way that is unpleasant.

7th
delve
delv
VERB

If you delve into a bag or a cupboard, you search inside it as if you are digging.

8th
alchemy
al-kum-ee

NOUN

Alchemy was a type of chemistry studied in the past, which tried to find ways to turn ordinary metals into gold.

* Alchemy comes from the Arabic word 'al-kīmiyā', which means 'transformation'.

9th
juror
joor-ur

NOUN

A juror is a member of a jury, which is a group of people who listen to the facts and decide the result of a trial in a court of law.

10th
dainty
dayn-tee

ADJECTIVE

Something that is dainty is small, delicate and pretty.

11th
prologue
pro-log

NOUN

The prologue is the part of a play, book or film that introduces the story.

12th
gallivant
gal-uh-vant

VERB

If you go gallivanting, you go out and have fun.

13th

dreich

dreek

ADJECTIVE

If the weather is dreich, it is dull and miserable. This is a Scottish word.

14th

cwtch

kutch

NOUN

Cwtch is a Welsh word for a cuddle.

TODAY IS VALENTINE'S DAY, AN ANNUAL FESTIVAL THAT CELEBRATES LOVE AND FRIENDSHIP.

15th
urban
ur-bun
ADJECTIVE

Urban means belonging to, or relating to, a city or a town.

* Urban comes from the Latin word 'urbs', which means 'city'.

16th
ephemeral
e-fem-ur-ul
ADJECTIVE

Something that is ephemeral lasts for only a short time.

* Ephemeral comes from the Greek word 'ephemeros', which means 'lasting for one day'.

17th
pontoon
pon-toon
NOUN

A pontoon is a floating platform, often used as a temporary bridge.

18th
logjam
log-jam
NOUN

A logjam is a difficult situation which has existed for a long time.

19th
cantankerous
kan-tan-kur-us
ADJECTIVE

Someone who is cantankerous is bad-tempered and complains a lot.

20th
revere
re-veer
VERB

If you revere someone, you respect and admire them.

¡HOLA!

Nǐ Hǎo

Ciao!

TODAY IS INTERNATIONAL MOTHER LANGUAGE DAY, WHICH AIMS TO PROTECT AND CELEBRATE ALL THE LANGUAGES OF THE WORLD.

21st
polyglot
po-lee-glot

NOUN

A polyglot is a person who speaks or understands many languages.

22nd
spellbinding
spel-bine-ding

ADJECTIVE

If something is spellbinding, it is so fascinating that you can think about nothing else.

23rd
plaid
plad

NOUN

Plaid is a woven material with a checked design of lines and squares.

*Plaid comes from a word in the Scottish Gaelic language.

24th
excavate
eks-kuv-ayt

VERB

When archaeologists excavate, they remove earth carefully from the ground to look for things that were used in the past.

25th
quintessential
kwin-tes-sen-shul

ADJECTIVE

If you describe something as quintessential, you mean it is a perfect or typical example of that thing.

26th
squall
skwawl

NOUN

A squall is a brief, violent storm.

TODAY IS INTERNATIONAL POLAR BEAR DAY, WHICH RAISES AWARENESS ABOUT THE IMPACT OF GLOBAL WARMING ON THESE SNOW-LOVING BEARS.

27th
chionophile
keye-on-uh-file

NOUN

A chionophile is an animal or plant that can live in cold, wintery conditions.

28th
zest
zest

NOUN

Zest is a feeling of great enthusiasm and energy.

29th
leapling
leep-ling

NOUN

A leapling is a person who is born on 29th February.

BONUS WORD!
TODAY IS A LEAP DAY, AN EXTRA DAY WHICH OCCURS EVERY FOUR YEARS ON 29TH FEBRUARY.

is for

MARCH

1st
okapi
o-ka-pee

NOUN

An okapi is an animal with a reddish-brown coat, small horns and horizontal white stripes on its legs.

* Okapi comes from a word in the Mvuba language of central Africa.

2nd
bibliophile
bib-lee-o-file

NOUN

A bibliophile is someone who loves or collects books.

* Bibliophile comes from the Greek words 'biblion', which means 'book', and 'philos', which means 'loving'.

ON WORLD BOOK DAY, CHILDREN DISCUSS BOOKS AND DRESS UP AS THEIR FAVOURITE CHARACTERS. IN THE UK IT IS CELEBRATED IN MARCH.

3rd
raconteur
ra-kon-tur

NOUN

A raconteur is someone who tells funny or interesting stories.

4th
festooned
fes-toond
ADJECTIVE

If something is festooned, it has lots of decorations hanging across it.

5th
scamper
skam-pur
VERB

If a person or an animal scampers, they move quickly with small, light steps.

6th
graciously
gray-shus-lee
ADVERB

If someone behaves graciously, they behave in a kind, polite and pleasant way.

7th
knave
nayv
NOUN

Knave is an old-fashioned word for a dishonest or untrustworthy man.

31

MARCH

TODAY IS INTERNATIONAL WOMEN'S DAY, WHICH HONOURS THE ACHIEVEMENTS OF WOMEN PAST AND PRESENT.

8th
suffragette
suf-ra-jet

NOUN

A suffragette was a woman at the beginning of the 20th century who campaigned for women to be given the right to vote.

*Suffragette comes from the Latin word 'suffragium', which means 'the right to vote'.

9th
foreshadow
for-sha-doe

VERB

If something foreshadows a future event or situation, it is a sign that it will happen.

10th
soliloquy
so-lil-o-kwee

NOUN

A soliloquy is a speech in a play made by a character who is alone on the stage.

11th
shearling
sheer-ling

NOUN

A shearling is a young sheep that has been shorn (had its wool cut off) for the first time.

12th
synchronicity
sin-kron-is-it-ee

NOUN

Synchronicity is when two similar events happen at the same time, even though the events are not related to each other.

TODAY IS PI DAY, WHEN PEOPLE CELEBRATE THEIR LOVE OF MATHS AND NUMBERS.

13th
ambiguous
am-big-yoo-us

ADJECTIVE

If a word or phrase is ambiguous, it is unclear because it has more than one possible meaning.

*Ambiguous comes from the Latin word 'ambiguus', which means 'going here and there'.

14th
ratio
ray-shee-o

NOUN

A ratio is the mathematical relationship between two groups, telling you how much bigger one is than the other.

15th
unperturbed
un-puh-turbd

ADJECTIVE

Unperturbed means not worried or troubled.

16th
gambit
gam-bit

NOUN

A gambit is a clever action that you take to try to gain an advantage in a situation or game.

17th
smithereens
smith-ur-eens

NOUN

If something is smashed or blown to smithereens, it is broken into very small pieces.

* Smithereens comes from a word in the Irish Gaelic language.

18th
indignantly
in-dig-nunt-lee

ADVERB

If you say something indignantly, you say it in an angry way because you think it is unfair.

19th
frontrunner
frunt-run-ur

NOUN

The frontrunner is the person who is most likely to win a race or competition.

20th

hygge

hoo-guh

NOUN

Hygge is a Danish word for the creation of a cosy environment that makes you feel happy and safe.

TODAY IS INTERNATIONAL DAY OF HAPPINESS, WHEN PEOPLE THINK ABOUT HOW TO MAKE THEMSELVES AND OTHERS HAPPY.

TODAY IS WORLD POETRY DAY, WHICH ENCOURAGES EVERYONE TO SHARE POETRY WITH FAMILY AND FRIENDS.

21st

haiku

heye-koo

NOUN

A haiku is a short Japanese poem with 3 lines and 17 syllables.

* Haiku comes from the Japanese words 'hai', which means 'amusement', and 'ku', which means 'verse'.

22nd

geyser

gee-zur

NOUN

A geyser is a hole in the ground from which hot water and steam shoot out.

* Geyser comes from a word in the Icelandic language.

23rd

intrepid

in-tre-pid

ADJECTIVE

Someone who is intrepid is brave and fearless.

35

24th
zany

zay-nee

ADJECTIVE

A zany person is odd in an amusing way.

25th
xanadu

zan-a-doo

NOUN

A xanadu is a beautiful or impressive place.

26th
melodramatic

mel-o-dram-a-tik

ADJECTIVE

If someone is being melodramatic, they are behaving in an exaggerated and overemotional way.

27th
accomplice

a-kum-plis

NOUN

An accomplice is a person who helps someone else to commit a crime.

28th
fondue
fon-doo

NOUN

Fondue is a dish made from a warm sauce – for example, melted cheese – into which you dip bread and other foods.

* **Fondue is a French word that means 'melted'.**

29th
philosophise
fil-os-o-fize

VERB

If someone is philosophising, they are thinking or talking about important ideas.

30th
nonchalantly
non-shul-ont-lee

ADVERB

If you behave nonchalantly, you behave in a calm and relaxed way, often showing that you do not care.

31st
diurnal
deye-ur-nul

ADJECTIVE

If you describe an animal as being diurnal, you mean that it is awake and active during the daytime.

is for

APRIL

1st
rapscallion
rap-skal-ee-on

NOUN

A rapscallion is an untrustworthy or mischievous person.

TODAY IS APRIL FOOLS' DAY, WHEN MISCHIEVOUS PEOPLE PLAY TRICKS ON EACH OTHER BEFORE DECLARING 'APRIL FOOL!'.

2nd
lachrymose
lak-ri-mose

ADJECTIVE

Lachrymose is a word used to describe someone who cries often and easily.

* Lachrymose comes from the Latin word 'lacrima', which means 'a tear'.

3rd
anachronistic
a-na-kron-ist-ik

ADJECTIVE

Anachronistic refers to something that belongs, or seems to belong, to another time in history.

* Anachronistic comes from the Greek word 'anakhronismos', which means 'a mistake about time'.

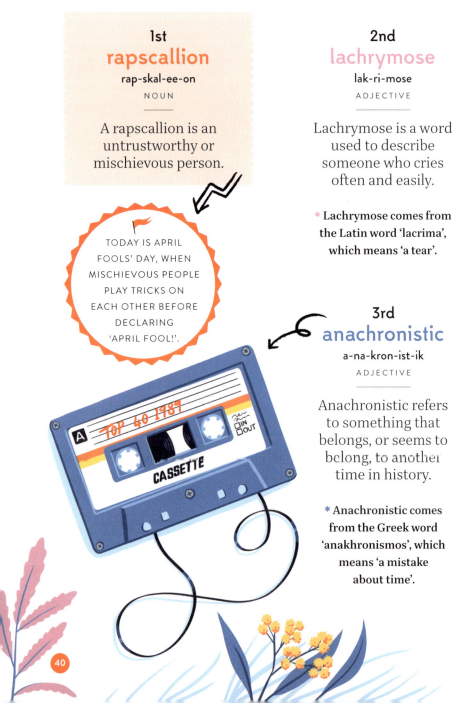

TOP 40 1989

A
IN
OUT

CASSETTE

4th
teem

teem

VERB

If a place is teeming with people, there are lots of people moving around inside.

5th
kaput

ku-put

ADJECTIVE

If you say that something is kaput, you mean that it is broken and useless.

6th
exodus

ek-so-dus

NOUN

An exodus is when a large number of people leave a place at the same time.

7th
teal

teel

ADJECTIVE

Something that is teal is dark greenish-blue in colour.

8th
octothorpe

ok-to-thorp

NOUN

An octothorpe is a hash (#) symbol.

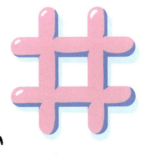

APRIL

9th
mythical
mith-i-kul
ADJECTIVE

Something that is mythical is imaginary or exists only in stories.

TODAY IS NATIONAL UNICORN DAY, WHEN PEOPLE TELL TALES ABOUT THESE MYSTERIOUS, MYTHICAL CREATURES.

10th
visceral
vis-ur-ul
ADJECTIVE

Visceral feelings are felt very deeply and you may find it difficult to control or ignore them.

11th
sustainable
su-stay-nu-bul
ADJECTIVE

Sustainable means using natural resources in a way that does not damage the environment.

TODAY IS INTERNATIONAL DAY OF HUMAN SPACE FLIGHT, THE ANNIVERSARY OF THE FIRST TIME A PERSON WENT INTO SPACE IN 1961.

12th
orbit
or-bit

VERB

When a satellite orbits a planet, moon or sun, it moves in a curving path around it.

* **Orbit comes from the Latin word 'orbis', which means 'circle'.**

13th
loquacious
lo-kway-shus

ADJECTIVE

Someone who is loquacious is very talkative.

* **Loquacious comes from the Latin word 'loqui', which means 'I speak'.**

14th
impulsively
im-puls-iv-lee

ADVERB

If you do something impulsively, you do it suddenly without thinking about it carefully first.

APRIL

15th
slew
sloo
NOUN

A slew is a large number of something.

* Slew comes from the Old Irish word 'slog', which means 'army'.

16th
alms
aams
NOUN

Alms is an old-fashioned word for gifts of money, food or clothing given to people who do not have much.

17th
sapling
sap-ling
NOUN

A sapling is a young tree.

18th
thriving
threye-ving
ADJECTIVE

Someone or something that is thriving is successful and developing well.

19th
gremlin
grem-lin
NOUN

A gremlin is a tiny, imaginary creature that gets inside things, especially machines, and makes them stop working.

20th
haberdashery
ha-bur-dash-ur-ee

NOUN

Haberdashery refers to the small items used for sewing, such as cloth, needles, thread and buttons.

21st
conscientious
con-shee-en-shus

ADJECTIVE

If you are conscientious, you follow the rules and work very hard.

TODAY IS EARTH DAY, WHEN PEOPLE TAKE ACTION TO PROTECT OUR PLANET FROM THREATS LIKE POLLUTION AND DEFORESTATION.

22nd
rewild
ree-wild

VERB

To rewild an area of land is to protect it and return it to its natural state – for example, by planting trees.

23rd
bard

bard

NOUN

A bard is a literary word for a poet.

24th
adjourn

a-jurn

VERB

If someone adjourns a meeting or trial, they pause it for a short time.

25th
kimono

ki-mo-no

NOUN

A kimono is a long, loose piece of traditional Japanese clothing with wide sleeves and a sash.

26th
initiate

in-ish-ee-ate

VERB

If you initiate something, you start it or cause it to happen.

27th
effervescent
ef-ur-ves-ent

ADJECTIVE

An effervescent liquid is one that releases small bubbles of gas.

28th
vegetti
vej-et-ee

NOUN

Vegetti is spaghetti made from thinly cut vegetables.

*Vegetti is a combination of the words 'vegetable' and 'spaghetti'.

29th
disconcerting
dis-kon-ser-ting

ADJECTIVE

If something is disconcerting, it makes you feel anxious or uncomfortable.

30th
verdant
ver-dunt

ADJECTIVE

A place that is verdant is covered with lush green grass, trees and plants.

*Verdant comes from the Latin word 'viridis', which means 'green'.

is for

MAY

MAY

1st
maypole
may-pole
NOUN

A maypole is a tall pole with long ribbons attached, which people dance around on 1st May.

TODAY IS MAY DAY, WHEN PEOPLE IN EUROPEAN CULTURES DANCE AND SING TO CELEBRATE THE BEGINNING OF SUMMER.

2nd
yearn
yern
VERB

If you yearn for something, you want it very much.

3rd
exquisite
ek-skwiz-it
ADJECTIVE

Something that is exquisite is very beautiful and delicate.

4th
droid
droyd
NOUN

In science fiction, a droid is a robot that looks like a human being.

HELLO!

TODAY IS STAR WARS™ DAY, WHEN PEOPLE CELEBRATE THE STAR WARS FILMS: MAY THE 4TH BE WITH YOU!

5th
rustic
rus-tik

ADJECTIVE

If something is rustic, it is simple and rough-looking in a way that is typical of the countryside.

* Rustic comes from the Latin word 'rus', which means 'countryside'.

6th
extroverted
eks-tro-vur-tid

ADJECTIVE

Someone who is extroverted is energetic and likes spending time with other people.

7th
ornamental
or-na-ment-ul

ADJECTIVE

Something that is ornamental is designed to be pretty rather than practical.

8th
borborygmus
bor-bur-ig-mus

NOUN

Borborygmus is the noise your tummy makes when it rumbles.

* Borborygmus comes from a word in the ancient Greek language.

9th
perishable
pe-rish-uh-bul

ADJECTIVE

If food is perishable, it is likely to go off after a short amount of time.

MAY

10th
odyssey
od-i-see

NOUN

An odyssey is a very long and exciting journey.

* 'The Odyssey' is a poem by the ancient Greek writer Homer, about an eventful voyage by a man called Odysseus.

11th
embody
em-bo-dee

VERB

To embody an idea or quality means to represent it or express it fully.

12th
verisimilitude
ver-iss-im-il-it-youd

NOUN

If a book or a film has verisimilitude, it feels true or real.

13th
divergent
deye-ver-junt

ADJECTIVE

Divergent things are different from each other.

14th
gargoyle
gar-goil

NOUN

A gargoyle is a stone carving of an ugly creature that is found on top of some old buildings.

* **Gargoyle comes from the Old French word 'gargouille', which means 'throat'.**

15th
grudgingly
gruj-ing-lee

ADVERB

If you do something grudgingly, you don't really want to do it.

16th
perambulation
per-amb-you-lay-shun

NOUN

Perambulation means walking about for pleasure.

FOR WALK TO SCHOOL WEEK, CHILDREN AROUND THE UK WALK TO SCHOOL FOR EXERCISE AND ENJOYMENT. IT HAPPENS EVERY YEAR IN MAY.

17th
askew
ask-you

ADJECTIVE

If something is askew, it is not straight.

18th
mulligrubs
mul-i-grubs

NOUN

In the southern United States of America, mulligrubs is another word for grumpiness or a bad mood.

19th
skulk
skulk

VERB

If you skulk, you move around quietly because you do not want to be seen.

20th
apiary
ay-pee-eh-ree

NOUN

An apiary is a place where bees are kept, usually in a collection of beehives.

* Apiary comes from the Latin word 'apis', which means 'bee'.

TODAY IS WORLD BEE DAY, WHICH HIGHLIGHTS THE IMPORTANCE OF BEES AND OTHER POLLINATORS FOR OUR ECOSYSTEM.

21st
ecotourism
ee-ko-toor-is-um

NOUN

Ecotourism is the business of organising holidays to places of natural beauty in a way that does not damage the environment.

22nd
conspicuous
kon-spik-you-us

ADJECTIVE

If something is conspicuous, you see it or notice it very easily.

* Conspicuous comes from the Latin word 'conspicio', which means 'I catch sight of'.

23rd
whimsical
wim-sik-ul

ADJECTIVE

If something is whimsical, it is unusual and playful, often in a funny way.

24th
blossom
bloss-um

NOUN

Blossoms are the delicate flowers that grow on fruit trees.

25th
assonance
ass-un-uns

NOUN

Assonance is when two syllables or sounds that are close together sound similar – for example, 'mystery' and 'mastery'.

26th
uncanny
un-can-ee

ADJECTIVE

If something is uncanny, it is strange and mysterious.

27th
protagonist
pru-tag-on-ist

NOUN

The protagonist is the main character in a play or story.

* **Protagonist comes from the Greek words 'protos', which means 'first', and 'agonistes', which means 'actor'.**

28th
fastidiously
fas-tid-ee-us-lee

ADVERB

If you do something fastidiously, you do it carefully and thoroughly because you want everything to be perfect.

29th
undertone
un-dur-tone

NOUN

If you say something in an undertone, you say it very quietly.

30th
azure
az-your

ADJECTIVE

Something that is azure is bright blue in colour.

* Azure comes from a Persian word for the name of a blue precious stone.

31st
yonder
yon-dur

ADVERB

Yonder is an old-fashioned word meaning 'over there'.

is for

JUNE

1st
celestial
sel-es-tee-ul

ADJECTIVE

Celestial means relating to the sky or outer space.

*Celestial comes from the Latin word 'caelum', which means 'heaven'.

2nd
karma
kar-muh

NOUN

In some religions, like Hinduism and Buddhism, karma is the belief that your actions in this life affect all your future lives.

*Karma means 'action' in Sanskrit, an ancient language that used to be spoken in India.

3rd
wistfully
wist-fu-lee

ADVERB

If you think wistfully about something, especially something you want but can't have, you think about it sadly.

4th
cumulus
kyou-myou-lus

NOUN

Cumulus is a type of fluffy white cloud that forms when hot air rises quickly, usually in summer.

5th
jeopardy
jep-ur-dee

NOUN

If something is in jeopardy, it is in danger of being damaged or destroyed.

6th
resilient
res-il-ee-unt

ADJECTIVE

Someone who is resilient is able to recover quickly from difficult events.

7th
cascade
kas-kayd

VERB

When water cascades down a waterfall, it flows very quickly and in large quantities.

* Cascade comes from the Italian word 'cascare', which means 'fall'.

8th
nurdle
nur-dul

NOUN

A nurdle is a very small pellet of plastic used in the production of larger plastic products.

TODAY IS WORLD OCEANS DAY, WHICH TEACHES PEOPLE HOW TO KEEP OUR OCEANS CLEAN OF NURDLES AND OTHER PLASTICS.

9th
objectively
ob-jek-tiv-lee

ADVERB

If you think about something objectively, you think about it in a way that is based on facts, rather than feelings.

10th
upcycle
up-seye-kul

VERB

If you upcycle something, such as an old piece of furniture or clothing, you repair and reuse it – often in a way that makes it more fashionable or valuable.

11th
bamboozle
bam-boo-zul

VERB

If you bamboozle someone, you confuse or trick them.

12th
infinitesimal
in-fin-it-es-i-mul

ADJECTIVE

Something that is infinitesimal is extremely small.

13th
ventriloquist
ven-tril-uh-kwist

NOUN

A ventriloquist is someone who can speak without moving their lips, to make it seem like their voice is coming from somewhere else, often a puppet.

14th
platelet
playt-let

NOUN

Platelets are small particles in the blood that help it to clot, which stops the bleeding if you hurt yourself.

TODAY IS WORLD BLOOD DONOR DAY. IT IS A CHANCE TO THANK EVERYONE WHO SAVES LIVES BY DONATING BLOOD.

15th
frangipani
fran-ji-pa-nee

NOUN

Frangipani is a tropical bush with white or pink flowers and a very strong, sweet smell.

＊ Frangipani is named after Marquis Muzio Frangipani, an Italian nobleman who invented a perfume that smelled like almonds.

16th
incorrigible
in-ko-rij-uh-bul

ADJECTIVE

If you say that a person's behaviour is incorrigible, you think that it is bad and cannot be changed or improved.

17th
mesmerise
mes-mur-eyes

VERB

If something mesmerises you, you are so interested in it that you cannot think about anything else.

18th
bask
bask

VERB

If you bask in the sunshine, you lie in it and enjoy the warmth.

19th
encapsulate
en-kap-syou-layt

VERB

To encapsulate an idea means to express or summarise its most important points.

20th
decant
di-kant

VERB

If you decant a liquid, you pour it from one container into another.

21st
symphony
sim-fu-nee

NOUN

A symphony is a long piece of classical music written to be played by an orchestra.

TODAY IS MAKE MUSIC DAY, WHEN PEOPLE ALL AROUND THE WORLD PLAY MUSIC TOGETHER. A GLOBAL SYMPHONY!

22nd
equilibrium
ek-wil-ib-ree-um

NOUN

Equilibrium is another word for balance.

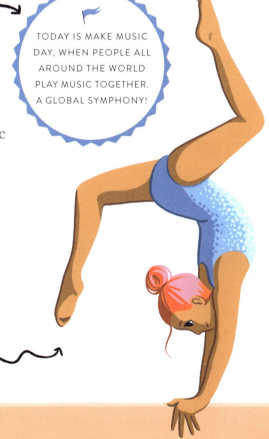

23rd
brae
bray
NOUN

Brae is a Scottish word for a hill or slope.

24th
humungous
hew-mung-gus
ADJECTIVE

Something that is humungous is extremely large.

25th
ironic
eye-ron-ik
ADJECTIVE

If you say something is ironic, you think it is interesting, strange or funny because it is the opposite of what you would expect.

26th
flabbergasted
flab-ur-gas-tid

ADJECTIVE

Someone who is flabbergasted is extremely surprised.

27th
lucid
loo-sid

ADJECTIVE

Lucid writing or speech is clear and easy to understand.

28th
galah
gu-laa

NOUN

A galah is an Australian bird with a pink breast and a grey back and wings.

✱ Galah comes from a word in the Yuwaalaraay language of eastern Australia.

29th
rejuvenate
ri-dyou-vu-nayt

VERB

If something rejuvenates someone, it makes them look or feel young again.

30th
wuthering
wuth-ur-ing

ADJECTIVE

Wuthering is a word used to describe the roaring sound made by a strong wind.

is for

JULY

1st
elongated
ee-long-gay-tid

ADJECTIVE

Something that is elongated is long and thin.

2nd
diaphanous
deye-a-fun-us

ADJECTIVE

Diaphanous fabric is so thin and delicate that you can almost see through it.

* Diaphanous comes from the Greek words 'dia', which means 'through', and 'phainein', which means 'show'.

3rd
consternation
kon-stur-nay-shun

NOUN

Consternation is a feeling of anxiety, annoyance or shock.

4th
perspective
pur-spek-tiv

NOUN

A perspective is a particular way of thinking about something.

5th
monsoon
mon-soon
NOUN

The monsoon is the season of very heavy rain that takes place during the summer in southern Asia.

6th
flippant
flip-unt
ADJECTIVE

Someone who is flippant is not being serious enough.

7th
moreish
mor-ish
ADJECTIVE

If you describe food as moreish, you mean that it is so tasty that you want to keep eating more of it.

8th
acquiesce
a-kwee-es
VERB

If you acquiesce in or to something, you agree to a plan or a suggestion, often unwillingly.

TODAY IS WORLD CHOCOLATE DAY, WHEN PEOPLE CAN INDULGE IN THIS MOREISH SWEET TREAT!

9th
flimsy
flim-zee

ADJECTIVE

If something is flimsy, it is made of very thin material and can be easily damaged.

10th
deftly
deft-lee

ADVERB

If you do something deftly, you do it quickly and skilfully.

11th
coral
ko-rul

NOUN

Coral is a spiky, brightly coloured substance that is formed in the ocean from the bones of small sea animals.

12th
juxtaposition
juk-stu-pu-zi-shun

NOUN

Juxtaposition is when you put two different words or ideas next to each other to highlight their differences – for example, the saying 'making a mountain out of a molehill'.

13th

retrospective

re-tru-spek-tiv

ADJECTIVE

If something is retrospective, it looks back on things that happened in the past.

* Retrospective comes from the Latin words 'retro', which means 'back', and 'specto', which means 'I look'.

14th

inquisitively

in-kwiz-i-tiv-lee

ADVERB

If you say something inquisitively, you are showing that you are curious and want to know more.

15th

portmanteau

port-man-toe

NOUN

A portmanteau is when you combine two words to make a new one – for example, 'brunch' is a combination of 'breakfast' and 'lunch'.

16th

encore

on-kor

NOUN

An encore is an extra performance given at the end of a show, played when the audience shouts for more.

* Encore is a French word that means 'again'.

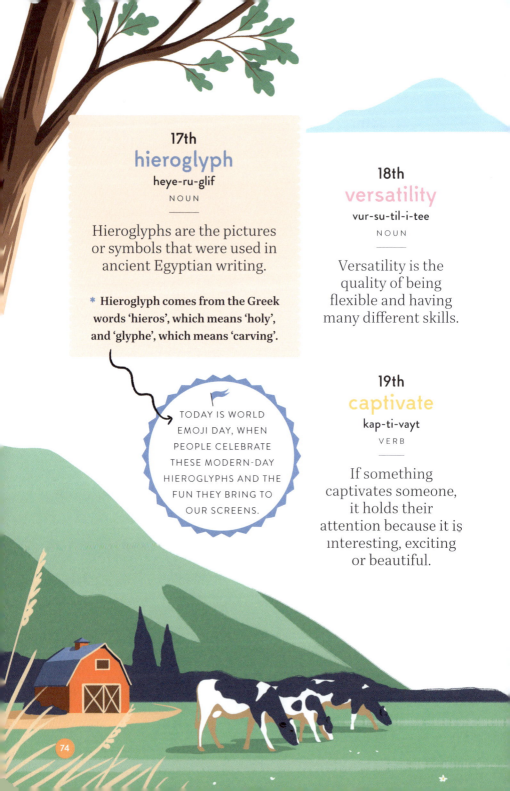

17th
hieroglyph
heye-ru-glif

NOUN

Hieroglyphs are the pictures or symbols that were used in ancient Egyptian writing.

* Hieroglyph comes from the Greek words 'hieros', which means 'holy', and 'glyphe', which means 'carving'.

TODAY IS WORLD EMOJI DAY, WHEN PEOPLE CELEBRATE THESE MODERN-DAY HIEROGLYPHS AND THE FUN THEY BRING TO OUR SCREENS.

18th
versatility
vur-su-til-i-tee

NOUN

Versatility is the quality of being flexible and having many different skills.

19th
captivate
kap-ti-vayt

VERB

If something captivates someone, it holds their attention because it is interesting, exciting or beautiful.

20th
echo
e-koe

NOUN

An echo is a sound that you hear more than once, because it bounces off a surface and comes back.

21st
tome
tome

NOUN

A tome is a very large and heavy book.

22nd
bucolic
bew-kol-ik

ADJECTIVE

Bucolic means relating to the countryside or country life.

* Bucolic comes from the Greek word 'boukolos', which means 'cowherd'.

23rd
solar
so-lur

ADJECTIVE

Solar is a word used to describe things that are related to the Sun.

* Solar comes from the Latin word 'sol', which means 'sun'.

75

TODAY IS AMELIA EARHART DAY, WHICH HONOURS THE FIRST FEMALE AVIATOR TO FLY SOLO ACROSS THE ATLANTIC IN 1932.

24th
aviator
ay-vee-ay-tur

NOUN

An aviator is the pilot of an aircraft.

* Aviator comes from the Latin word 'avis', which means 'bird'.

25th
transient
tran-zee-unt

ADJECTIVE

Something that is transient lasts for only a short time.

26th
noctambulist
nok-tam-bew-list

NOUN

A noctambulist is someone who walks in their sleep.

27th
zephyr
ze-fur

NOUN

A zephyr is a gentle wind.

28th
rendezvous

ron-day-voo

NOUN

A rendezvous is an arrangement to meet someone at a particular time and place, often in secret.

* Rendezvous comes from the French language.

TODAY IS INTERNATIONAL DAY OF FRIENDSHIP, WHICH CELEBRATES THE BONDS BETWEEN PEOPLE, COUNTRIES AND CULTURES.

30th
empathise

em-path-eyes

VERB

If you empathise with someone, you understand how they are feeling.

29th
talon

ta-lun

NOUN

Talons are the strong, hooked claws on birds of prey (birds that kill other creatures for food).

31st
balmy

baa-mee

ADJECTIVE

Balmy weather is warm and pleasant.

is for

AUGUST

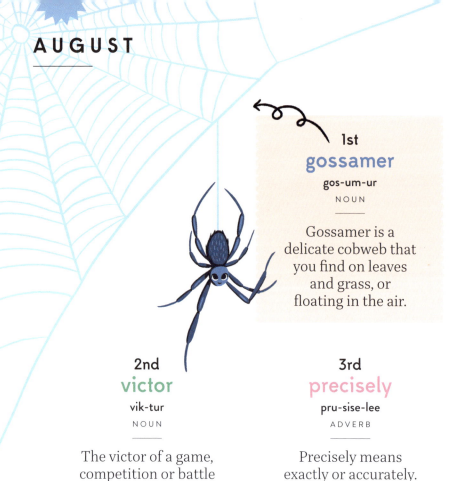

1st
gossamer
gos-um-ur

NOUN

Gossamer is a delicate cobweb that you find on leaves and grass, or floating in the air.

2nd
victor
vik-tur

NOUN

The victor of a game, competition or battle is the winner.

3rd
precisely
pru-sise-lee

ADVERB

Precisely means exactly or accurately.

4th
cerulean
sur-oo-lee-un

ADJECTIVE

Something that is cerulean is deep blue in colour.

5th
oxymoron
ok-see-more-on

NOUN

An oxymoron is when you use two words together that have opposite meanings – for example, 'loud whisper'.

6th
jujitsu
joo-jit-soo
NOUN

Jujitsu is a Japanese sport and form of self-defence, in which two people try to knock each other down using only their strength and skill.

* **Jujitsu comes from the Japanese words 'ju', which means 'gentleness', and 'jutsu', which means 'art'.**

7th
parched
parcht
ADJECTIVE

If you are parched, you are very thirsty.

8th
wanderlust
won-dur-lust
NOUN

Wanderlust is a strong desire to travel around the world.

* **Wanderlust comes from the German language.**

9th
esplanade
es-plan-ayd

NOUN

An esplanade is a long, wide path where people walk for pleasure, especially one that is by the sea.

10th
picturesque
pik-chur-esk

ADJECTIVE

Somewhere that is picturesque is very pretty and charming.

11th
barter
bar-tur

VERB

If you barter something or with someone, you swap one thing for another, rather than selling it for money.

12th
wholeheartedly
hole-har-tid-lee

ADVERB

If you do something wholeheartedly, you do it completely and enthusiastically.

13th
agility
aj-il-i-tee

NOUN

Someone's agility is their ability to move quickly and easily.

TODAY IS INTERNATIONAL LEFT HANDERS DAY, WHEN LEFT-HANDED PEOPLE CAN CELEBRATE THEIR UNIQUENESS.

14th
glitch
glich

NOUN

A glitch is a small problem which stops something from working properly.

15th
scorcher
skor-chur

NOUN

A scorcher is a very hot and sunny day.

TODAY IS NATIONAL TELL A JOKE DAY IN THE USA, THE PERFECT TIME TO SHARE SOME LAUGHS WITH YOUR LOVED ONES.

16th
jester
jes-tur

NOUN

In medieval Europe, a jester was an entertainer whose job it was to tell jokes and do silly things to make people laugh.

17th
soporific
sop-ur-if-ik
ADJECTIVE

Something that is soporific makes you feel sleepy.

18th
evoke
iv-oke
VERB

If something evokes a particular memory or feeling, it makes you think about it.

TODAY IS INTERNATIONAL ORANGUTAN DAY, WHICH PROMOTES THE CONSERVATION OF THESE ARBOREAL ANIMALS.

19th
arboreal
ar-bor-ee-ul
ADJECTIVE

Arboreal animals live mainly in trees.

* Arboreal comes from the Latin word 'arbor', which means 'tree'.

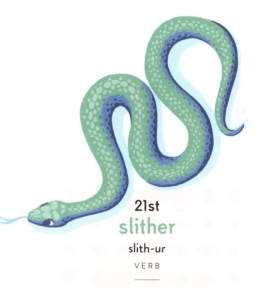

20th
crescendo
kresh-en-doe

NOUN

A crescendo is when a sound, especially a piece of music, gets louder and louder.

* **Crescendo is an Italian word that means 'increasing'.**

21st
slither
slith-ur

VERB

When a snake slithers, it moves smoothly along the ground, sliding from side to side.

22nd
genealogy
jeen-ee-al-uj-ee

NOUN

Genealogy is the study of family history, showing how different members of a family are related to one another.

23rd
galore
gu-law

ADJECTIVE

You use galore to emphasise that something exists in very large amounts – for example, this book has words galore!

24th
oasis
oh-ay-sis
NOUN

An oasis is a small area in a desert where water and plants are found.

25th
doppelganger
dop-ul-gang-ur
NOUN

Your doppelganger is someone who looks exactly like you (but is not related to you).

*Doppelganger comes from the German words 'doppel', which means 'double', and 'ganger', which means 'goer'.

26th
tamarind
tam-ur-ind
NOUN

A tamarind is a tropical evergreen tree that grows edible fruit and sweet-smelling flowers.

27th
dapple
dap-ul

VERB

If sunlight dapples a surface, it creates patches of light and shade.

28th
ingenious
in-jeen-ee-us

ADJECTIVE

An ingenious idea is one that is very clever and innovative.

29th
vermilion
vur-mil-ee-un

ADJECTIVE

Something that is vermilion is bright red in colour.

30th
gobbledygook
gob-ul-dee-gook

NOUN

Gobbledygook is language that is impossible to understand because it seems like nonsense or is very complicated.

31st
fragile
fraj-eyel

ADJECTIVE

If something is fragile, it can be easily broken or damaged.

* Fragile comes from the Latin word 'frango', which means 'I break'.

is for

SEPTEMBER

1st
cursive
kur-siv
ADJECTIVE

Cursive handwriting is written with rounded, joined-up letters.

TODAY IS WORLD LETTER WRITING DAY, SO PICK UP A PEN AND PAPER, AND PRACTISE YOUR CURSIVE HANDWRITING!

2nd
renovate
ren-uh-vayt
VERB

If someone renovates an old building, they repair and improve it.

3rd
pitcher
pitch-ur
NOUN

A pitcher is a large jug.

4th
waltz
wolts
NOUN

A waltz is a formal dance in which two people hold each other and spin elegantly around a ballroom, to a piece of music with a 1–2–3 rhythm.

5th
guesstimate
ges-ti-mayt

NOUN

A guesstimate is an approximate calculation that is based mainly on guesswork, because you do not know all the facts.

*Guesstimate is a combination of the words 'guess' and 'estimate'.

6th
kittiwake
ki-tee-wayk

NOUN

A kittiwake is a seabird with white feathers, pale grey wings with black tips, and a square-shaped tail.

*These birds are named after the noise they make, a shrill call that sounds like 'kitteee-waaake'!

7th
paradigm
par-uh-deyem

NOUN

A paradigm is a very clear or typical example of something, explaining how it works or showing how it can be made.

*Paradigm comes from the Greek word 'paradeigma', which means 'pattern'.

8th
lackadaisical
lak-uh-days-ik-ul

ADJECTIVE

If someone is lackadaisical, they do not seem interested in, or enthusiastic about, what they are doing.

SEPTEMBER

9th
gait
gayt

NOUN

Someone's gait is their particular way of walking.

10th
quizzically
kwiz-ik-uh-lee

ADVERB

If you look at someone quizzically, you show that you are surprised or amused by their behaviour.

TODAY IS MINDFULNESS DAY, WHEN PEOPLE THINK ABOUT THE PRESENT MOMENT AS A WAY OF STAYING CALM AND RELAXED.

11th
collywobbles
ko-lee-wob-uls

NOUN

If you have the collywobbles, you feel very nervous and queasy.

12th
equanimity
e-kwan-im-i-tee

NOUN

Equanimity is a calm state of mind and a peaceful attitude to life.

13th
ochre
o-kur
ADJECTIVE

Something that is ochre is yellowish-orange in colour.

14th
deciduous
de-sid-you-us
ADJECTIVE

A deciduous tree is one that loses its leaves in autumn every year and grows new ones in the spring.

* Deciduous comes from the Latin word 'decidere', which means 'fall down'.

15th
laconic
lak-on-ik
ADJECTIVE

Someone who is laconic uses very few words to say something.

16th
gruel
groo-ul
NOUN

Gruel is a cheap and simple food made by boiling oats in water or milk.

17th
haywire
hay-weye-er
ADJECTIVE

If something goes haywire, it goes out of control or starts doing the wrong thing.

18th
yesteryear
yes-tur-yeer

NOUN

You use yesteryear to refer to a time in the past, often in a fond or nostalgic way.

TODAY IS TALK LIKE A PIRATE DAY, WHEN LADS AND LASSIES PRETEND TO BE PIRATES. YO, HO, HO!

19th
doubloons
dub-loons

NOUN

Doubloons are Spanish gold coins that were used in the 17th and 18th centuries, when piracy at sea was common.

20th
vault
volt

NOUN

A vault is a secure room where money and other valuable things can be kept safely.

21st
utopia
you-toe-pee-a

NOUN

A utopia is an imaginary place where everything is perfect and everyone is happy.

* Utopia comes from the Greek words 'ou', which means 'not', and 'topos', which means 'a place'.

TODAY IS INTERNATIONAL DAY OF PEACE, WHICH STRIVES TO RESOLVE CONFLICT BETWEEN COUNTRIES AND MAKE THE WORLD A MORE EQUAL PLACE.

22nd
rhetorical
ret-or-i-kul

ADJECTIVE

A rhetorical question is asked in order to make a point, and therefore does not need an answer – for example, 'do you think money grows on trees?'.

23rd
escalate
es-ku-layt

VERB

If a situation escalates, it becomes worse.

24th
phantasmagorical
fan-taz-mu-gor-i-kul

ADJECTIVE

Phantasmagorical means very strange, like something in a dream.

25th
yucca
yu-ka
NOUN

A yucca is a tropical plant with spiky leaves and white, bell-shaped flowers.

* **Yucca comes from a word in the Taino language of the Caribbean.**

26th
dubious
dyou-bee-us
ADJECTIVE

If you are dubious about something, you are not completely sure about it.

27th
shrewdly
shrood-lee
ADVERB

If you act shrewdly, you are able to understand a situation quickly, then use that understanding to your advantage.

28th
thwart
thwort
VERB

If you thwart someone, you stop them from doing something or getting what they want.

29th
incognito
in-kog-nee-toe
ADJECTIVE

Someone who is incognito is using a false name or wearing a disguise to avoid being recognised.

30th
avatar
av-ut-ar
NOUN

An avatar is an image that represents you on screen in an online game or chatroom.

is for

OCTOBER

1st
skein

skayn

NOUN

———

A skein is a length of thread, especially wool or silk, wound loosely around itself.

2nd
inglenook

in-gul-nook

NOUN

———

An inglenook is a Scottish word for a cosy seat beside a fireplace.

3rd
renewables

re-nyou-ub-uls

NOUN

———

Renewables are sources of energy that are good for the environment, because they are made from resources that nature can replace – for example, solar power from the Sun.

4th
zoology

zoo-ol-uh-jee

NOUN

———

Zoology is the scientific study of animals.

TODAY IS WORLD ANIMAL DAY, WHICH AIMS TO IMPROVE THE LIVES OF ANIMALS AROUND THE WORLD.

5th
pedagogy
ped-uh-goj-ee
NOUN

Pedagogy is the study of the methods and principles of teaching.

* **Pedagogy comes from the Greek words 'pais', which means 'child', and 'agogos', which means 'leader'.**

6th
biosphere
beye-us-feer
NOUN

The biosphere is all parts of the Earth's surface and atmosphere where there are living things – from high up in the sky, to deep down in the ocean.

7th
jostle
jos-ul
VERB

If someone jostles you, they bump into you roughly, usually in a crowd of people.

8th
mither
mi-thur
VERB

If you mither, you moan about something or make a fuss.

9th
myriad
mir-ee-ud

NOUN

A myriad of people or things is a very large number of them.

* Myriad comes from the Greek word 'murias', which means 'ten thousand'.

10th
rambunctious
ram-bunk-shus

ADJECTIVE

A rambunctious person is very energetic in a cheerful and noisy way.

11th
introverted
in-tro-vur-tid

ADJECTIVE

Someone who is introverted is quiet and shy, and likes spending time alone.

12th
gargantuan
gar-gan-choo-un

ADJECTIVE

Something that is gargantuan is enormous.

13th
agog
a-gog

ADJECTIVE

If you are agog, you are excited about something and eager to find out more about it.

14th
ornithologist
or-ni-tho-lu-jist

NOUN

An ornithologist is someone who studies birds.

WORLD MIGRATORY BIRD DAY TAKES PLACE IN OCTOBER AND CALLS FOR THE GLOBAL CONSERVATION OF THESE LONG-DISTANCE TRAVELLERS.

15th
fervent
fer-vunt

ADJECTIVE

Someone who is fervent has strong feelings about something.

16th
eccentric
ik-sen-trik

ADJECTIVE

If you describe someone as eccentric, you think they behave, speak or dress in an unusual way.

17th
infuse
in-fyous

VERB

If something infuses you with an emotion like happiness, you feel that emotion very strongly.

18th
cacophony
ku-kof-uh-nee

NOUN

A cacophony is an unpleasant mixture of loud sounds.

* Cacophony comes from the Greek words 'kakos', which means 'bad', and 'phone', which means 'sound'.

19th
gryphon
griff-un

NOUN

A gryphon is a mythical creature with the head and wings of an eagle and the body of a lion.

20th
scrumptious
skrump-shus
ADJECTIVE

If you describe food as scrumptious, you mean that it tastes extremely good.

21st
diva
dee-va
NOUN

A diva is a famous female singer, especially in opera.

* **Diva is an Italian word that means 'goddess'.**

22nd
conundrum
ku-nun-drum
NOUN

A conundrum is a confusing and difficult problem.

23rd
swiftly
swift-lee
ADVERB

Something that happens swiftly happens very quickly or immediately.

24th
hoodwink
hood-wink
VERB

If someone hoodwinks you, they trick or deceive you.

OCTOBER

25th
glean
gleen
VERB

If you glean information, you collect it slowly and often with difficulty.

OCTOBER IS DYSLEXIA AWARENESS MONTH, WHICH CELEBRATES NEURODIVERSITY AND SHARES STORIES ABOUT WHAT IT'S LIKE TO LIVE WITH DYSLEXIA.

26th
neurodiversity
nyou-roe-deye-vur-si-tee
NOUN

Neurodiversity is the idea that people think and behave in different ways, and these differences are a normal part of human life.

27th
quixotic
kwik-so-tik
ADJECTIVE

If you think that someone's plans are quixotic, you think that they are unrealistic and impractical.

* Quixotic comes from the name of the hero in an old Spanish novel called 'Don Quixote'.

28th
ghostwriter
goest-reye-tur
NOUN

A ghostwriter is someone who writes a book on behalf of the person who is named as the author.

29th
susurration
su-su-ray-shun
NOUN

Susurration is a soft whisper, murmur or rustling sound.

30th
yurt
yurt
NOUN

A yurt is a circular tent with a wooden frame, traditionally covered with felt or animal skins.

TODAY IS HALLOWEEN, WHEN PEOPLE DRESS UP, CARVE PUMPKINS AND SHARE SPOOKY STORIES!

31st
eerie
eer-ee
ADJECTIVE

Something that is eerie is strange and a bit scary.

is for

NOVEMBER

1st
vicarious
veye-kair-ee-us

ADJECTIVE

A vicarious feeling is experienced by watching, listening to, or reading about other people doing something, rather than by doing it yourself.

2nd
hither
hith-ur

ADVERB

Hither is an old-fashioned word meaning towards this place, so 'come hither' was used to say 'come here'.

3rd
hirsute
her-syoot

ADJECTIVE

Someone who is hirsute is hairy.

4th
impeccable
im-pek-ub-ul

ADJECTIVE

If someone's behaviour or appearance is impeccable, it is perfect.

'MOVEMBER' IS A CHARITY EVENT THAT HAPPENS EVERY NOVEMBER, WHEN PEOPLE GROW MOUSTACHES TO RAISE AWARENESS AND MONEY FOR MEN'S HEALTH ISSUES.

5th
pyrotechnics
peye-roe-tek-niks

NOUN

Pyrotechnics is the art of making or setting off fireworks.

* Pyrotechnics comes from the Greek words 'pur', which means 'fire', and 'tekhne', which means 'skill'.

TODAY IS BONFIRE NIGHT (OR GUY FAWKES NIGHT) IN THE UK, WHEN FIREWORKS LIGHT UP THE NIGHT SKY.

6th
discombobulated
dis-kum-bob-you-lay-tid

ADJECTIVE

If you are discombobulated, you are confused and unsettled.

7th
convoluted
kon-vul-oo-tid

ADJECTIVE

If you say that something is convoluted, you think it is unnecessarily complicated and difficult to understand.

8th
keepsake
keep-sayk

NOUN

A keepsake is a small present that reminds you of a particular person or event.

9th
brace
brase

VERB

If you brace yourself for something unpleasant, you get ready to deal with it.

10th
parchment
parch-munt

NOUN

In the past, parchment was the skin of an animal, such as a goat, that was used for writing on.

11th
hypothetical
heye-pu-thet-ik-ul

ADJECTIVE

If something is hypothetical, it is based on possible ideas or situations, rather than on real ones.

12th
xebec
zee-bek

NOUN

A xebec is a small Mediterranean ship with three masts, used in the past by pirates.

13th
diya
dee-ya

NOUN

A diya is a small oil lamp, usually made from clay.

* Diya comes from the Hindi language.

14th
gazillion
gu-zi-lee-un

NOUN

A gazillion is an extremely large number or amount.

15th
cravat
kruv-at

NOUN

A cravat is a wide piece of folded cloth that is worn around the neck like a tie.

* **Cravat comes from a French word meaning 'Croatian', because cravats used to be worn by Croatian soldiers in the French army.**

16th
efficacious
ef-ik-ay-shus

ADJECTIVE

Something that is efficacious is successful at getting the result you want.

17th
ubiquitous
you-bik-wi-tus

ADJECTIVE

If you describe something as ubiquitous, you mean that it is common and seems to be everywhere.

18th
cerise
su-rees

ADJECTIVE

Something that is cerise is bright reddish-pink in colour.

19th
deteriorate
di-teer-ee-ur-ayt

VERB

If something deteriorates, it gets worse.

TODAY IS WORLD CHILDREN'S DAY, WHICH STRIVES TO CREATE A BETTER FUTURE FOR CHILDREN EVERYWHERE.

21st
palindrome
pa-lin-drome

NOUN

A palindrome is a word or phrase that is the same whether you read it forwards or backwards – for example, 'kayak'.

* Palindrome comes from the Greek words 'palin', which means 'again', and 'dromos', which means 'running'.

20th
nurture
nur-chur

VERB

If you nurture a young child, you protect them and look after them carefully.

22nd
spontaneously
spun-tay-nee-us-lee

ADVERB

If you do something spontaneously, you do it suddenly and without planning.

23rd
enigma
in-ig-mu

NOUN

An enigma is a person or thing that is mysterious or difficult to understand.

24th
lax
laks

ADJECTIVE

If you describe someone as lax, you mean that they are not careful or strict enough.

25th
soiree
swa-ray

NOUN

A soiree is a fancy party held in the evening.

* **Soiree comes from the French word 'soir', which means 'evening'.**

26th
footloose
foot-loose

ADJECTIVE

If you describe someone as footloose, you mean that they have no responsibilities and are free to do whatever they want, and go wherever they want.

27th
kerfuffle
kur-fuf-ul

NOUN

A kerfuffle is a lot of fuss, noise or excitement.

28th
resoundingly
ru-zownd-ing-lee

ADVERB

If something is done resoundingly, it is done in a complete and clear way.

29th
neologism
nee-ol-uh-jiz-um

NOUN

A neologism is a newly invented word or phrase in a language, or a new meaning for an existing word or phrase – for example, 'staycation' has come to mean a holiday (or 'vacation') where you stay in the local area.

30th
mistpouffer
mist-poo-fur

NOUN

A mistpouffer is a loud booming sound that seems to come out of the fog over a lake or river.

31st
serendipity
se-run-dip-i-tee

NOUN

Serendipity is the luck some people have in finding interesting or valuable things by chance.

is for

DECEMBER

1st
zenith

zen-ith

NOUN

The zenith of something is the time when it is at its most successful or powerful.

2nd
tenacious

ten-ay-shus

ADJECTIVE

Someone who is tenacious is determined and does not give up easily.

3rd
slate

slayt

NOUN

Slate is a dark grey rock that splits easily into thin layers and is often used for covering roofs.

4th
duel

dyou-ul

NOUN

In the past, a duel was a formal fight arranged between two people to settle an argument.

TODAY IS INTERNATIONAL VOLUNTEER DAY, WHICH ENCOURAGES PEOPLE TO BE SELFLESS AND HELP OTHERS.

5th
philanthropic
fil-an-thro-pik

ADJECTIVE

Someone who is philanthropic is generous and gives money to help people in need.

*Philanthropic comes from the Greek words 'philos', which means 'loving', and 'anthropos', which means 'human'.

6th
charisma
kur-iz-mu

NOUN

If someone has charisma, they are able to attract or influence people with their personality and natural charm.

7th
amulet
am-you-lit

NOUN

An amulet is a small object or piece of jewellery that you wear or carry for good luck.

8th
vapid
va-pid

ADJECTIVE

Someone or something that is vapid is dull and uninteresting.

9th
kinaesthetic
kin-iss-thet-ik

ADJECTIVE

If you are a kinaesthetic learner, you learn best through touch and movement.

10th
urgently
ur-junt-lee

ADVERB

If something needs to be done urgently, it needs to be done as soon as possible because it is very important.

11th
vertiginous
ver-tij-in-us

ADJECTIVE

A vertiginous cliff or mountain is very high and steep.

12th
guinea
gi-nee

NOUN

A guinea is an old British coin, worth about one pound in today's money.

* Guinea comes from the name of the country in Africa, because gold from here was used to make coins at the time.

TODAY IS INTERNATIONAL MOUNTAIN DAY, WHICH EDUCATES PEOPLE ON HOW TO LOOK AFTER OUR MIGHTY MOUNTAINS.

13th
hiraeth
hee-reyeth

NOUN

Hiraeth is a Welsh word meaning a deep sense of longing for a place that you can never go back to.

14th
hunky-dory
hung-kee-door-ee

ADJECTIVE

If you say that everything is hunky-dory, you mean that everything is fine and pleasant.

15th
parliament
par-lu-munt

NOUN

Parliament is the collective name for a group of owls.

16th
luminous
loo-min-us

ADJECTIVE

Something that is luminous gives off bright light.

* Luminous comes from the Latin word 'lumen', which means 'light'.

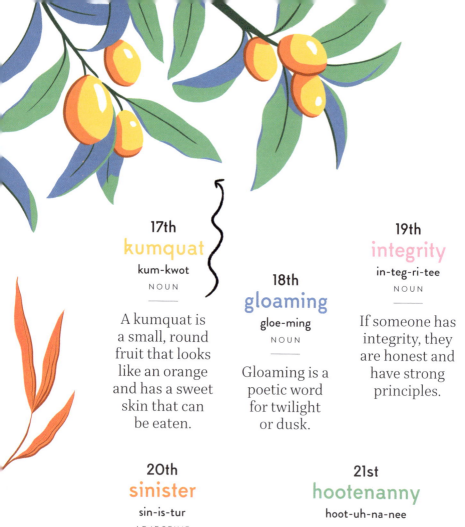

17th
kumquat
kum-kwot

NOUN

A kumquat is a small, round fruit that looks like an orange and has a sweet skin that can be eaten.

18th
gloaming
gloe-ming

NOUN

Gloaming is a poetic word for twilight or dusk.

19th
integrity
in-teg-ri-tee

NOUN

If someone has integrity, they are honest and have strong principles.

20th
sinister
sin-is-tur

ADJECTIVE

Something that is sinister seems harmful or evil.

* Sinister is a Latin word that means 'left'. In ancient Roman times, the left-hand side was considered unlucky.

21st
hootenanny
hoot-uh-na-nee

NOUN

A hootenanny is a performance by folk singers.

22nd
wreath
reeth

NOUN

A wreath is an arrangement of flowers and leaves in the shape of a circle, often used as a decoration.

23rd
peruse
pu-rooz

VERB

If you peruse something, you read it, especially to find something you are interested in.

24th
tintinnabulation
tin-tin-ab-you-lay-shun

NOUN

Tintinnabulation is the ringing sound of bells.

DECEMBER

25th
exuberance
ig-zyou-bur-uns

NOUN

Exuberance is behaviour that is full of energy, excitement and cheerfulness.

TODAY IS CHRISTMAS DAY, A CHRISTIAN RELIGIOUS FESTIVAL COMMEMORATING THE BIRTH OF JESUS, WHICH IS ALSO WIDELY CELEBRATED BY NON-CHRISTIANS AS A TIME FOR BEING WITH FAMILY.

26th
delicacy
de-li-kas-ee

NOUN

A delicacy is a rare or expensive food that is especially nice to eat.

27th
epiphany
eh-pi-fu-nee

NOUN

An epiphany is a moment when you suddenly understand something important.

28th
incandescent
in-kan-des-unt

ADJECTIVE

Something that is incandescent gives out a lot of light when it is heated.

29th
serenade
se-run-ayd

VERB

If you serenade someone you love, you sing or play music to them, traditionally outside their window.

* **Serenade comes from the Italian word 'sereno', which means 'peaceful'.**

30th
coorie
coor-ee

VERB

If you coorie into someone, you snuggle into them. This is a Scottish word.

TODAY IS NEW YEAR'S EVE, WHEN PEOPLE CELEBRATE THE END OF THE YEAR AND LOOK FORWARD TO THE START OF ANOTHER!

31st
jamboree
jam-bu-ree

NOUN

A jamboree is a large party or celebration where there are lots of people enjoying themselves.

The End